# SMART STRATEGIES FOR INVESTING WISELY AND SUCCESSFULLY

FINANCIAL SECURITY AND LIFE SUCCESS FOR TEENS™

# SMART STRATEGIES FOR
# INVESTING WISELY AND SUCCESSFULLY

## JUDY MONROE PETERSON

ROSEN
PUBLISHING®

New York

Published in 2015 by The Rosen Publishing Group, Inc.
29 East 21st Street, New York, NY 10010

**Library of Congress Cataloging-in-Publication Data**

Peterson, Judy Monroe.
Smart strategies for investing wisely and successfully/Judy
Monroe Peterson. — First Edition.
        pages cm. — (Financial security and life success for teens)
Audience: Grades 7-12.
Includes bibliographical references and index.
ISBN 978-1-4777-7618-6 (library bound) —
ISBN 978-1-4777-7620-9 (pbk.) —
ISBN 978-1-4777-7621-6 (6-pack)
1. Finance, Personal—Juvenile literature. 2. Investments—
Juvenile literature. I. Title.
HG179.P44728 2014
332.6—dc23

2013049324

*Manufactured in the United States of America*

# CONTENTS

INTRODUCTION

S aving and investing are ways for everyone, including teens, to make their money work for them. Money deposited in a savings account at a bank or credit union is very safe because the federal government protects it. In return for this security, people earn only a little interest. They can take the chance of making more money than in savings accounts by buying bonds, stocks, or mutual funds. Investments offer greater monetary rewards than savings but are riskier because the federal government does not insure them. Investors could lose some or all of their money if they do not make reasonable investment decisions.

Before investing, everyone needs a road map, or plan, for building wealth. The place to start is for young people to determine their financial goals in life. Everyone's financial objectives are different. One person may want to pay to go to college, while another hopes to travel around Europe in two years. All long-term, expensive financial goals require a financial plan. Creating and following this plan is key to managing money now and later in life.

Following some time-tested investing strategies can be a great way to grow money. One of the most basic guidelines is that the earlier people begin to invest, the more money they can possibly make over their lifetime. They can invest on their own, get help from a local bank, or hire a money manager to handle their bonds, stocks, or mutual funds. Individuals can buy or sell bonds, stocks, and mutual funds

Establishing healthy saving and investing habits at an early age can help young people reach financial success throughout their life. Knowing how to secure financial well-being is critical.

at the age of majority, which is eighteen in most states. Younger teens can get started investing nice and early by opening a custodial account with a parent or guardian for joint ownership of an investment.

Knowing how to invest is an important money-management skill to build wealth. Yet, a lot of young people are not taught these skills at home or school. Many parents, guardians, or other adults have little understanding of the basic concepts of investing, so they're unprepared to teach young investors those concepts. Although some teens may learn money skills at school, many U.S. schools are not doing an adequate job of providing financial literacy to their students, either. In 2013, Champlain College's Center for Financial Literacy graded the schools of each state based on how well they were helping their students to become financially literate. Only 40 percent of the state schools rated above average, earning an A or a B. Others did a mediocre or poor job of teaching personal money management. Sixty percent were graded as C or below, and of that number, more than 40 percent had a D or F. That leaves most young people to develop investment strategies on their own.

Teens can learn and practice financial skills, even if they are not taught at home or in school. However, some individuals jump into the investment world without much understanding of how it works. This reckless approach may cause anyone to quickly lose money. With wise strategies at the ready, young people can become as confident with investing as they are with their computers. Keep reading to learn how to reach your financial goals and start prospering as your wealth increases.

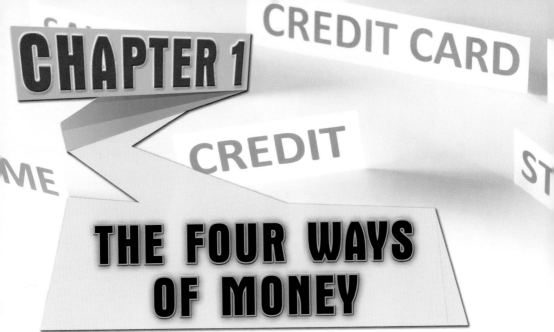

# CHAPTER 1

# THE FOUR WAYS OF MONEY

Everyone has four choices for how they can handle their money: Earn it, spend it, save it, or invest it. Knowing how to do those things are essential money-management skills. Young people can earn money by working at a part-time job. And everyone likes to spend it! Saving and investing make money do the work. Sound investments help everyone, including teens, reach their financial goals in life. Many adults invest so that they'll have money to relax or be comfortable when it comes time for retirement. Before jumping into buying bonds, stocks, or mutual funds, successful investors define their financial goals and then develop a financial plan to reach them.

## SETTING FINANCIAL GOALS

The key to investing is determining what is important in one's life. Making a wish list of what one plans to do in the

10

future is an excellent way to get started. Beginning investors can brainstorm what they want to accomplish in the next month, year, five years, or beyond, and then write down their ideas or put them on a computer program or website. All goals, even those that seem impossible to achieve, are OK. There are no right or wrong investment goals. Many people then set their list aside for a week or so to mull it over and make any changes. In addition, teens can ask friends, family members, or teachers to make suggestions about identifying sensible and reasonable financial goals.

The next step is to assign each goal into one of three categories: short term (six to twelve months), medium term (thirteen to twenty-four months), and long term (more than five years). An example of a short-term goal is buying a smartphone in nine months, whereas a medium-term goal is paying for a trip to England with friends in eighteen months. Long-term goals cover things further into the future, like having enough money to make a down payment on a house. Sometimes people add a fourth category for immediate goals (before six months), such as buying a school jacket in two months. Taking a few days to think about goals and priorities can be helpful.

Setting financial goals puts people in charge of their money. It's a positive habit and a great way for people to think proactively about their lives.

# ANTHONY'S FUTURE GOALS

WHEN ANTHONY WAS EIGHT YEARS OLD, HIS MOTHER TOOK HIM TO AN AIR SHOW AT A NEARBY AIRPORT. HE WAS AMAZED WHEN THE JET PILOTS FLEW SOMERSAULTS, AND HE DECIDED TO BECOME A JET PILOT. NOW, AT AGE SEVENTEEN, HE WORKS PART-TIME CLEANING INTERIORS OF PLANES AND DREAMS ABOUT FLYING. HIS GIRLFRIEND, AGE EIGHTEEN, PLANS TO BE A SOCIAL WORKER. THE FOLLOWING IS PART OF ANTHONY'S FINANCIAL PLAN TO REACH HIS TOP GOALS:

| GOAL | | COST | TIME WHEN NEEDED |
|---|---|---|---|
| IMMEDIATE (LESS THAN 6 MONTHS) | VIDEO GAME CONFERENCE | $100 | 5 MONTHS |
| SHORT TERM (1 YEAR) | NEW TABLET | $500 | 13 MONTHS |
| MEDIUM TERM (5-10 YEARS) | PROFESSIONAL PILOT, AAS DEGREE | $11,000 TUITION & FEES | 60 MONTHS |
| | BUY ENGAGEMENT RING | $3,500 | 78 MONTHS |
| LONG TERM (10 YEARS) | BUY NEW CAR | $23,000 | 126 MONTHS |
| | BUY HOUSE | $50,000 DOWN PAYMENT | 168 MONTHS |

TO REACH HIS GOALS, ANTHONY IS DEVELOPING A BUDGET TO SAVE AND INVEST HIS MONEY.

# MAKING THINGS HAPPEN: A FINANCIAL ACTION PLAN

A financial plan is actually an action plan, or a budget, for making financial goals happen. Good budgeting is what helps teens reach their money goals. A sensible budget can help them save, spend, and invest their money. After all, investing first requires earning, then saving money.

Making a budget is a multistep process and takes some time and effort to set up. But the results are well worth it.

Many tools exist to help put together a financial plan and its corresponding budget, including resources at the website of the Securities and Exchange Commission (www.investor.gov).

Without a budget, it's hard to know how much money you have and what you can spend. Following these five steps helps create and maintain a budget:

1.  Make a list of all income over four weeks. Income includes wages from a part-time job, an allowance from a parent or guardian, or money gifts for birthdays and other special occasions. Some people make money from a hobby, such as selling homemade holiday wreaths at a local farmers' market.

2.  At the same time, record all fixed expenses, which are payments that stay the same from month to month. Financial advisers highly recommend paying yourself first, which means putting savings first on your fixed list. They advise older teens to save 15 to 20 percent of their monthly income. For instance, someone with a yearly income of $4,050 can put about $61 to $81 into savings every month. Because younger teens have smaller incomes, they can aim for 10 percent. Other fixed expenses may include car payments, smartphone bills, and school activity fees. A good budget should include an emergency fund. Each month, everyone can set money aside to prepare for unexpected events like car repairs.

3.  Log in variable expenses on a separate list while recording fixed expenses. Variable expenses change from month to month, including gas for a car, clothing, sports equipment, and donations to a local animal shelter.

4.  Subtract all the fixed and variable expenses from the income. Surprises may pop up at this point. One teen might discover that she is not saving enough money to pay for

soccer camp in two months and also buy a prom dress in six months. Another young person may be spending more than he is earning.

5. Review the budget regularly and keep it up to date. As their needs change, investors change their goals and priorities to help them spend, save, and invest their money successfully.

# OVERCOMING OVERSPENDING

Overspending can be managed in three ways. One option is to work more hours at a job or provide a personal service, such as house cleaning, to earn extra money. A second possibility is to reduce spending, especially impulse buying. Finally, both can be done—increase income and cut expenses. The real secret to saving is to spend less than your income.

Besides working a part-time job for wages or getting an allowance, young people can increase their income by providing a service, such as cleaning an attic or garage. They may weed gardens, mow and trim lawns, shovel snow, walk dogs, babysit, or tutor. Some individuals enjoy selling homemade products, including bird feeders or jewelry. Another possibility is to sell things that are no longer needed for cash using websites such as eBay or Craigslist. Many used items are in demand, such as sporting gear, newer cell phones and other electronics, clothing, or musical instruments.

Sometimes people borrow money from friends or family when they have run through their own income. Borrowed

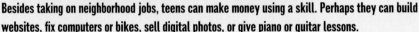
Besides taking on neighborhood jobs, teens can make money using a skill. Perhaps they can build websites, fix computers or bikes, sell digital photos, or give piano or guitar lessons.

money is a loan and a debt to be repaid. Anyone, including teens, can get into serious financial trouble by owing large amounts of money. If an entire credit card bill is not paid in full by its due date, the remaining balance is charged a high interest rate. Paying off that debt then becomes a bigger challenge. Creating and following a realistic financial plan to avoid borrowing money requires some time, effort, and discipline. The end results can help young people grow their money and build a stronger financial future.

# MYTHS AND FACTS

**MYTH:** INVESTING IS A QUICK WAY TO BECOME WEALTHY.

**FACT:** INVESTING IS NOT A GET-RICH-FAST SCHEME. INSTEAD, SUCCESSFUL INVESTORS TAKE A LONG-TERM APPROACH. THEY MAY KEEP THE SAME STOCK FOR YEARS, EVEN DECADES.

**MYTH:** YOU HAVE TO BE RICH TO START INVESTING.

**FACT:** MANY PEOPLE BEGIN INVESTING WITH SMALL AMOUNTS OF MONEY, SUCH AS $25 OR $50 A MONTH. ALTHOUGH MORE THAN HALF OF ALL ADULTS HAVE INVESTMENTS, VERY FEW LIVE IN MANSIONS OR OWN A PRIVATE JET.

**MYTH:** GETTING WEALTHY THROUGH INVESTING IS A COMPLEX PROCESS THAT MOST TEENS CANNOT ACHIEVE.

**FACT:** YOUNG PEOPLE CAN BUILD WEALTH BY TAKING A SERIES OF SMALL STEPS TO ACCOMPLISH THEIR FINANCIAL PLAN OVER TIME. EVERYONE TAKES A DIFFERENT PATH TO REACH HIS OR HER FINANCIAL GOALS.

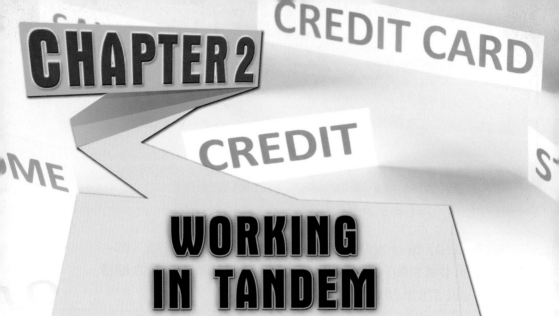

# CHAPTER 2

## WORKING IN TANDEM

S avings and investing go hand in hand because investments can't happen without savings. Banks offer everyone a safe holding place for keeping their money, and the federal government insures the money in savings accounts. Individuals can withdraw funds from their accounts to pay for things that they want later on.

## SAVVY SAVINGS ACCOUNTS

Many people store some of their money in a bank or credit union savings account. These accounts are a secure place to keep cash that they will need soon. We are less tempted to spend money we have put away. Interest rates on money deposited in savings accounts are very low.

---

Because money market deposit accounts are very liquid, they usually return a lower yield than other less liquid, longer-term cash investments, such as certificates of deposits (CDs).

Banks offer other savings products, including money market accounts and certificates of deposits (CDs). A money market account pays a bit more interest than a savings account, but savers are required to make a large deposit and keep a minimum balance. CDs require that money is deposited for a specific amount of time, such as three or twelve months, but they earn more interest than savings and money market accounts. Although it's possible to take money out of a CD before the given time is up, banks charge a large fee for early withdrawal.

It's not practical or safe to haul big, heavy bags of dollar bills around a mall to buy clothing and shoes. Instead, people use checks as a substitute for paper money and coins. Checks are safer and less awkward than lugging around lots of money everywhere we go. In addition, many employers automatically deposit wages into a checking account. Worried about being too young? Don't be. Numerous banks will set up a free checking account for teens with a cosigner, usually a parent or guardian. A checking account comes with a debit card, which works like a credit card except it withdraws funds from the checking account. When young people use a debit card to buy concert tickets, for example, the cash is immediately deducted, or taken, from their checking account balance.

People of all ages manage their savings accounts online. They can link to a bank using laptops, tablets, smartphones, or other mobile devices. Web-based tools are a terrific way to easily monitor savings and spending activities. You can check balances, view statements, transfer money between accounts, and pay bills. Banks may charge fees for some online services.

Everyone with a paper or online savings or checking account should keep a sharp eye on their banking activities. Banks charge an overdraft fee when more money is spent than the available account balance. This oversight can quickly become an expensive waste of money.

## STARTING WITH PAPER CHECKS

WHEN SOMEONE OPENS A NEW CHECKING ACCOUNT, BANKERS RECOMMEND USING PAPER CHECKS AS A WAY TO LEARN ABOUT THE FINANCIAL WORLD. GETTING TO KNOW YOUR PERSONAL BANKER IS A GOOD IDEA. THESE PROFESSIONALS ARE THERE TO SUPPORT YOU. THEY CAN EXPLAIN HOW A CHECKING ACCOUNT WORKS, WHAT INFORMATION IS ON CHECKS, AND HOW TO WRITE THEM. BANKERS CAN ALSO EXPLAIN HOW TO BALANCE A CHECKING ACCOUNT AND READ A BANK STATEMENT, WHICH IS A MONTHLY RECORD OF ALL DEPOSITS AND WITHDRAWALS ON THE ACCOUNT. LATER, MANY YOUNG PEOPLE DECIDE TO DO THEIR BANKING ONLINE.

# POWERFUL COMPOUNDING

Saving deposits and investments both allow money to work through the fantastic advantage of compounding. With compounding, you earn interest on the money you save or invest and on the interest the money earns, which is called compound interest. The extra dollars can add up over time because money is earned on a bigger and bigger pool of money.

Compounding is so amazing that even a small amount of dollars can add up to big money. Say that someone spends $3 a day on a candy bar and an energy drink for one year.

A compounding period can be daily, weekly, monthly, quarterly, or annually. The more frequent the compounding, the higher the yield because each time the principal grows, it earns more interest.

That adds up to $1,095 (not to mention quite a pile of candy wrappers and empty cans). Instead, the individual decides to put that $1,095 into a savings account earning 5 percent per year. At the end of one year, the amount will grow to $1,151, which is the original amount plus an extra 5 percent, or $56. The total would increase to $1,405 in five years, and $3,812 in twenty-five years.

Time unlocks the valuable power of compounding. The longer you wait to save and invest for the future, the longer you postpone the great advantage of compounding your money.

# INSIDIOUS INFLATION

Inflation reduces the purchasing power of every dollar. Say someone bought sunglasses at a store in the mall for $12.50 one year ago. Twelve months later, the same sunglasses now sell for $12.75. That is a 2 percent increase over the original price.

$12.50 × .02 = $0.25
$12.50 + $0.25 = $12.75

The higher price is because of inflation. When inflation rises, the price for everything goes up: clothing, baseball tickets, video games, and food. In 2013, the U.S. Bureau of Labor Statistics reported that the national rate of inflation was 2 percent and estimated the annual rate to be 2.2 to 2.3 percent until 2022. Inflation nibbles away at your money as prices keep increasing over time.

Even the price of a simple pair of sunglasses can rise significantly over a year. Inflation can ruin your financial plan if its long-term influences are not factored in.

Stuffing dollars under a mattress may seem like a good way to deal with rising costs. However, you will never have more money than what is stashed at home. The money does not earn interest and cannot keep up with inflation. As a result, dollar bills hidden away will buy less and less in the future.

# INTELLIGENT, INFORMED INVESTMENT RISK

Keeping up with inflation requires making wise decisions with savings and investments. Although both can earn interest money, only investments have the potential to increase faster than inflation. Unlike bank savings, investments carry varying levels of risk. Investing is essential to helping people reach their future financial goals. Bonds can also help preserve the spending power of someone's money.

 Risk tolerance relates to the degree that risk influences one's choice of investments. The degree of risk someone will accept will affect his or her potential return.

Governments and companies offer investors the chance to make their money grow faster instead of keeping it all in a savings account. Because the federal government does not insure investments, though, people could lose some or all of their capital.

Everyone handles investment risk differently. An individual might purchase only federal government bonds for complete safety, while someone else may focus on high-risk stocks, hoping for a hefty reward. Most people, including teens, rate their risk tolerance as somewhere in the middle. Wise investors increase their chance of success by making intelligent and informed investments based on their financial goals and plan. They never make hasty decisions about buying bonds, stocks, mutual funds, or real estate, such as a house.

Some people own collectibles as investments. Buying items for a collection is fun and exciting, but beware! Investing in coins, antiques, art, sports memorabilia, toys, or comic book collections is very risky. It may be easy to buy collectibles, but selling them for a profit is usually difficult.

# CHAPTER 3

## ULTRA SAFE AND VERY SAFE

**M**any beginning investors start on their path to riches by buying bonds. They have plenty of choices because many different organizations sell them to raise money. Corporate bonds are riskier than federal or municipal bonds but offer higher interest rates.

## BOND BASICS

When investors buy bonds, a government or an organization pays them a fixed rate of interest on their money. It also promises to return the money on a set date. Basically, a bond is an I owe you (IOU) between a lender and a government or corporation. These investments can be sold at any time. In addition, any earned interest is usually exempt from state and local taxes, so individuals owning government bonds keep more of their income in the long run.

Financial counselors usually advise people of all ages to own bonds. They are less risky than stocks and provide a safe,

Bond sales provide cash to help state and local governments borrow money for public works, such as the building of this overpass extension for the New Jersey Turnpike.

stable income even during difficult financial times. These investments offer a little higher interest rate than any of the bank savings products. As a rule, the longer the maturity of a bond, the higher the interest rate it pays.

Bonds may seem like the perfect investment, but they're not necessarily a good fit for everyone. Because a bond's value stays the same, investors do not build equity, and the earned interest may not keep up with inflation over time. Also, because these investments usually have low interest rates, the investor pockets only a small return when the bonds are redeemed.

Someone owning a federal savings bond or other types of U.S. bonds helps pay for national expenses. State, county, and city governments sell municipal bonds to finance large community projects, including new highways, hospitals, airports, and water treatment facilities. Your school was probably built with money raised from bonds. If companies want to build a new manufacturing building and offices, they may sell corporate bonds to obtain the necessary cash.

## THE REALITY OF BOND RISKS

ANYONE LOOKING FOR ULTRA-SAFE INVESTMENTS CAN PURCHASE SAVINGS BONDS AND OTHER U.S. BONDS. THE FEDERAL GOVERNMENT BACKS THEM, WHICH GIVES PEOPLE TREMENDOUS CONFIDENCE THAT THEIR LOANS WILL BE REPAID. MUNICIPAL BONDS ARE ALSO SUPER SAFE. ALTHOUGH IT RARELY HAPPENS, A STATE OR LOCAL GOVERNMENT MIGHT BE UNABLE TO PAY INTEREST TO ITS LENDERS. ALSO, CORPORATE BONDS CAN BE SAFE, OR THEY MIGHT JUST AS EASILY BE RISKY. WISE INVESTORS KEEP A CLOSE EYE ON THE RATINGS, OR SCORES, THAT MOODY'S INVESTORS SERVICE ASSIGNS TO BONDS. MOODY'S IS A BOND RATING COMPANY. SAFE BONDS EARN HIGH RATINGS.

# U.S. SAVINGS BONDS AND FEDERAL TREASURIES

If you own a U.S. savings bond, you own part of the federal government. Congratulations! Savings bonds are popular gifts for birthdays and other special occasions. They are a nifty way

American bonds and notes are often purchased by foreign countries that consider the U.S. government a safe investment. The same opportunity is available to you.

to invest long term, although they can be traded before or after their maturity date. Investors only need $25 to buy a series EE or a series I savings bond, which are purchased for face value. This means that someone who buys a face-value bond of $25 will receive $25 when it is redeemed. Series EE pay a fixed rate of interest for the length of the borrowing time, while the interest rate of series I bonds changes every May and November.

The government issues other U.S. bond series, including bills, notes, and bonds, known as treasuries. The two differences among the bonds are the minimum amount of purchase money and when they mature. Compared to savings bonds, bills mature at lightning speed. Individuals with short-term goals may purchase bills because they pay out in four to fifty-two weeks. Notes mature in two to ten years, and bonds in thirty years.

U.S. bonds are purchased directly from the government's TreasuryDirect website (http://www.treasurydirect.gov). All transactions and interest payments for U.S. bonds must be done online. Minors can own savings bonds, but only someone older than eighteen can buy them.

# CHECK OUT MUNICIPAL AND CORPORATE BONDS

Many of the things people see and use in their communities were financed with government, or municipal, bonds. Some high-income investors find these bonds particularly attractive

# JADA'S SAVINGS BONDS

JADA'S GRANDPARENTS BOUGHT HER A BOND FOR EACH OF FIVE YEARS. SHE WANTS TO KNOW THE TOTAL AMOUNT OF INTEREST EARNED WHEN ALL FIVE BONDS MATURE. FIRST, SHE MADE THIS TABLE:

| FACE AMOUNT OF BOND | PURCHASE DATE | INTEREST RATE | MATURITY DATE | TOTAL INTEREST EARNED AT MATURITY |
|---|---|---|---|---|
| $5,000 | 5/30/2009 | 7.51% | 5/30/2019 | $3,755 |
| $2,000 | 5/30/2010 | 6.80% | 5/30/2020 | $1,360 |
| $5,000 | 5/30/2011 | 5.50% | 5/30/2021 | $2,750 |
| $10,000 | 5/30/2012 | 6.55% | 5/30/2017 | $3,275 |
| $2,000 | 5/30/2013 | 7.10% | 5/30/2018 | $710 |

THEN SHE DETERMINED THE EARNED INTEREST AT MATURITY FOR THE 2009 BOND.

$5,000 × 7.51% = $375 IN ONE YEAR
$375 × 10 = $3,750 IN TEN YEARS

AFTER REPEATING THESE STEPS FOR THE REMAINING BONDS, JADA ADDED UP ALL OF THE EARNED INTEREST, ARRIVING AT A GRAND TOTAL OF $11,850. THE EARNED INTEREST OF $11,850 PLUS THE BONDS' FACE VALUE OF $22,000 MEANS THAT HER TOTAL AVAILABLE CASH WILL BE $33,850.

because they do not pay federal taxes on government interest payments. As a result, they keep all of their interest earnings. Municipal bonds, though, usually pay lower interest rates than most federal bonds.

All bonds are similar, except that a corporate bond means that people are lending money to a corporation. Beginning investors may find that corporate and municipal bonds are out of their reach because the minimum purchase is usually $5,000. They must use a brokerage company to buy these bonds.

Financial counselors advise young people to avoid junk bonds. Companies in financial trouble issue them, promising to pay a very high return. If the business improves, bond-holders can earn a lot of money. The truth is that many of these corporations are likely to fail. Then borrowers do not receive any interest and may also lose their capital.

# CHAPTER 4

# WHERE THE ACTION IS

When comedian Will Rogers (1879–1935) was asked about stock investing, he replied, "Buy stocks that go up, and if they don't, don't buy 'em." Everyone wishes his advice was easy to follow. Unfortunately it's not that simple, so most people buy and sell these investments through a brokerage firm. Successful stock investors are smart, patient, and willing to take thoughtful risks.

## DEMYSTIFYING STOCKS

Some people dream about owning the Coca-Cola Company, AT&T, or another large corporation. That goal may be unrealistic for most individuals. But everyone can own part

---

Will Rogers was a beloved actor, newspaper columnist, and radio commentator with more than sixty million listeners. Savvy and astute, he used humor to offer sound advice about money matters.

of a company by buying its stocks. Microsoft, McDonald's, and other giant corporations have millions of stocks and thousands of shareholders.

Investors can make money from stocks by receiving dividend payments. A successful company increases in value over time, sending its stock prices and dividends up. However, a business that does not grow loses value, causing its stock price and profits to drop. Shareholders may lose their dollars. Another way that investors can earn money is by purchasing stocks at a low price and then selling them at a higher price. This profit is called a capital gain.

Although the federal government does not guarantee stocks, many people purchase them. They take this risk because stocks have a long history of outperforming bank savings accounts, CDs, and bonds. For instance, from 1928 until 2010, the average annual return for government bonds was 3.7 percent, while stocks averaged 11 percent. Stocks are where the action is!

# WHAT'S FOR SALE ON THE STOCK MARKETS

Stock markets are centers for buying and selling stocks. They offer someone the chance to buy a slice of a company in exchange for taking on the risk of that investment. In the United States, most stocks are traded on the New York Stock Exchange (NYSE) and the National Association of Securities Dealers Automated Quotations (NASDAQ).

The NYSE, located on Wall Street in Manhattan, is a fast-paced, noisy place as floor traders shout out "Buy!" and

The New York Stock Exchange is the world's largest stock exchange. Brokers buy and sell shares of stock from many large American corporations and companies headquartered outside the United States.

"Sell!" with rapidly rising and falling stock prices. These brokers trade stocks for their investors. Many of their transactions take place using software programs, but they also conduct business face to face.

NASDAQ holds the honor of being the first global electronic stock market in the world. Because it is entirely on the Internet, someone can buy or sell from anywhere around the globe. A large number of technology companies trade on NASDAQ, including Apple, Microsoft, and Facebook.

# DECIPHERING STOCK TABLES

Savvy investors take the time to research a company and its stock before making any purchases. They may start by reading stock tables, which contain a lot of useful information. Financial newspapers, like the *Wall Street Journal*, and websites provide these charts.

The listings may look confusing at first, but potential investors can quickly learn what they mean. Each stock has a ticker symbol (an abbreviation), such as SUNENV for the Sunny Environmental Company. The symbols are listed alphabetically. A simplified stock listing for this business and what the terms mean may look like this:

## SUNNY ENVIRONMENTAL STOCK LISTING

| 52-WK | | | | | | | |
| High | Low | Stock (Div) | Yld% | P/E | Sales 100s | Last | Chg |
| 42.25 | 37.52 | SUNENV (.40) | 1.4 | 18 | 5978 | 43.20 | +1.30 |

- **52-Week High/Low** Highest and lowest stock prices one year ago.
- **Stock** A code for a company's name. If dividends are paid, the amount (Div) is next to the stock name.
- **Yld %** Return on stockholder's investment.

- **P/E** Price-to-earnings ratio, or the share price divided by the company's earnings per share. The higher the P/E, the more investors will pay for the stock.
- **Sales 100s** Number of stocks traded the previous day multiplied by 100.
- **Close** Stock price when the trading day ended. This number rises over time for successful companies.
- **Last** Final stock price for the previous day.
- **Chg** Difference between today's closing price and the previous day's closing price.

# SPOTTING STOCK MARKET INDICATORS

You might hear people say, "The Dow went up thirty points yesterday," or "The stock market closed down today." They are actually talking about a stock market index, which tracks the daily performance of stocks from well-established companies. It provides a snapshot of how well the stock market is doing.

The two best-known indices are the Dow Jones Industrial Average (Dow) and the S&P 500 index. The Dow measures the stock performance of thirty large and successful U.S. corporations, such as American Express and General Electric. It reports the number of points a stock rises or falls. Each point is equal to $1 per share, which means that if a stock rises by five points, its price increases by $5. The S&P 500 reflects the performance of the top 500 U.S. companies.

The Dow and S&P 500 reflect the ups and downs of the general economy. When the market is trending upward, people

## DISCOVERING DIVIDENDS

GOOD INVESTING IN THE STOCK MARKET MEANS MAKING MONEY FROM DIVIDENDS. A COMPANY MIGHT PAY DIVIDENDS AS CASH, WHICH PROVIDES PEOPLE WITH INCOME. FIGURING OUT THE AMOUNT OF A DIVIDEND PAYMENT IS SIMPLE. FOR EXAMPLE, IF A COMPANY DECLARES A DIVIDEND OF $67, AN INDIVIDUAL WITH 10 SHARES GAINS $670 (10 × $67), WHILE SOMEONE WITH 1,000 SHARES RECEIVES $67,000 (1,000 × $67). DIVIDENDS ARE USUALLY PAID FOUR TIMES A YEAR. ALL STOCKS ARE RISKY. NO MATTER HOW WELL A COMPANY HAS DONE IN THE PAST, ITS FUTURE DIVIDENDS MAY INCREASE, STAY THE SAME, DECREASE, OR DISAPPEAR.

call it a bull market and feel optimistic about future business conditions. A bear market exists if they are pessimistic about the economy, which sends the stock market downward.

# TYPES OF STOCK

Investors can choose from a variety of stocks to reach their long-term goals. High-risk growth stocks are not for the faint-hearted. They do not pay dividends, and some are very high risk because their prices change rapidly and erratically. People buying these stocks hope to get large share prices over time. Growth businesses are usually in new or fast-growing industries, such as high technology.

Walt Disney, Coca-Cola, AT&T, and American Express all have something in common. These companies sell blue-chip stocks that have moderate growth in earnings. Shareholders

Blue-chip stocks, like Walt Disney, are sold by corporations that have a long history of profitable operation. These stocks hold or increase value during economic recessions and boom times.

should expect regular dividends that steadily increase over time. Huge, international, well-established companies sell these stocks, and they have a long track record of paying dividends regularly.

Utility companies often sell income stocks that deliver consistent dividends to their investors. They can do this because everyone regularly uses electricity, water, gas, and other utilities. Utility and other income companies grow slowly but pay high dividends.

Stocks are great investments for long-term goals. Most people buy and sell them through a brokerage company.

# CHAPTER 5

# POOLS OF MONEY

Some people want to own stocks in many different companies. Unfortunately that would require a lot of money, which they may not have. Instead, everyone can make their wish come true by buying mutual funds, which are investments made up of dozens or even hundreds of different stocks or bonds. Anyone with a small amount of money can purchase shares of a mutual fund. Every fund offers different levels of risk and opportunities to earn money.

## BRING ON THE BENEFITS OF MUTUAL FUNDS

"I love mutual funds," wrote Jane Bryant Quinn in her book, *Making the Most of Your Money Now*. She is a nationally known counselor who helps people manage their personal finances. Many other experts agree with Quinn.

A mutual fund is an investment in which individuals pool

Trusted by millions, expert Jane Bryan Quinn provides solid, basic advice on personal finances in her books and regular columns. Her own investments are mostly index mutual funds.

their money to buy a collection of money markets, bonds, stocks, or other assets. Investors own shares in that fund and pay a professional financial manager to keep track of everything in the collection. Many people find that owning a mutual fund is a cheaper and more effective way of owning a large group of bonds or stocks, instead of buying each investment separately.

Like Quinn, lots of people like mutual funds. In 2012, the Investment Institute Company estimated that ninety-two million individuals in the United States owned them. Mutual funds make it easy to diversify because someone's dollars are spread across a large number and wide variety of securities. Diversification may help individuals lower their investment

## INVESTMENTS THAT MAKE A DIFFERENCE: SOCIALLY RESPONSIBLE FUNDS

IF INVESTORS DECIDE TO PUT THEIR DOLLARS TO WORK IN COMPANIES THAT FOCUS ON MAKING A DIFFERENCE IN THE WORLD, THEY CAN CHOOSE SOCIALLY RESPONSIBLE MUTUAL FUNDS. MANAGERS FOR THESE FUNDS DO NOT INVEST IN INDUSTRIES SUCH AS TOBACCO, ALCOHOL, GAMBLING, WEAPONS, OR NUCLEAR POWER. THEY ALSO RULE OUT BUSINESSES THAT POLLUTE THE ENVIRONMENT OR VIOLATE HUMAN RIGHTS. A GOOD PLACE TO BEGIN SLEUTHING FOR THESE TYPES OF FUNDS IS ONLINE, AT THE SOCIALFUNDS WEBSITE (WWW.SOCIALFUNDS.COM).

risk of major losses if share values fall. Conversely, a skillful fund manager who selects profitable companies can increase the value of the fund's shares and the total value of the shareholders' investment—and that makes everyone happy. Mutual funds are also very liquid, meaning they can easily be bought and sold.

Most prospective investors can discover a fund of interest because banks, credit unions, brokerage firms, and investment companies offer thousands of them. Each fund has a specialty, which may be a specific industry, such as technology, environmental protection, or health care. Some funds focus on municipal or corporate bonds, while others invest in large, small, or new companies.

# SPECIFIC TYPES OF MUTUAL FUNDS

Some people find it difficult to choose from the enormous number of available mutual funds. To help narrow their options, they can look at specific types of funds, including money markets, bonds, stocks, balanced funds, or index funds. Money market funds focus on short-term, low-risk investments, such as CDs and Treasury bills. Someone stashing away dollars to meet a short-term goal of six to twelve months may think about investing in money markets.

The remaining types of mutual funds are intended for investors who plan to hold them for many years. Investors might use them for long-term goals, such as paying for an education or buying a home. Someone may buy bond funds to get a regular income from dividends. In contrast, individuals hoping to make more money over time may choose stock funds. Balanced funds offer something for everyone because they combine bonds and stocks into a single fund. Index funds are different from other funds. The managers of these funds invest in stocks that match a financial index, such as the Dow Jones Industrial Average, S&P 500, or NASDAQ.

# MASTERING MUTUAL FUND INVESTING

Potential investors should take the time to study the prospectus of a fund before buying its shares. This legal document may take some time to read through. However, it contains essential facts about a fund, including its investment strategy, performance history, and fees. Individuals can use this information to help them decide if a fund fits their budget and financial goals.

To invest in a mutual fund, people first choose a fund company and then decide which group of investments they want to purchase. Some companies offering fund management include Fidelity, Vanguard, Charles Schwab, and T. Rowe Price. They then select a mutual fund and pay the investment firm a specific amount of money to open an account. Although an initial payment can be as low as $250, they usually cost $1,000 to $5,000.

It's important to know how load and no-load fees affect someone's initial investment. For a load mutual fund, everyone pays an up-front fee—and that reduces the amount of their

The U.S. Securities and Exchange Commission requires mutual funds to include specific types of information in every prospectus. Key data must be presented in a standard, easy-to-read format.

initial investment. Say an individual invests $5,000 in a load fund with an initial fee of 5 percent ($5,000 × 4% = $200). In reality, the investment is $4,800 ($5,000 - $200 = $4,800). No-load funds do not require an initial fee, which means someone's full $5,000 immediately goes to work for him or her.

# MAKING SENSE OF MUTUAL FUND TABLES

In addition to reading a fund's prospectus, everyone can study mutual fund tables in financial newspapers like the *Wall Street Journal* and financial websites. Every table may look a little different, but they all provide the same key facts. To start, potential investors look for the abbreviation of a fund's name. These symbols are organized alphabetically. A fund listing contains the following information:

## SAFE WORLD MUTUAL FUND LISTING

| 52-WK | | | | |
| --- | --- | --- | --- | --- |
| High | Low | NAV | Net Chg | YTD % Chg |
| 10.71 | 10.12 | $11 | +0.20 | 1.5 |

**52-Week High and Low** is the fund's highest and lowest value during the previous fifty-two weeks.

**NAV** means the net asset value (NAV), or the price of one fund share.

**Net Chg** is the net change in the previous day. A positive number means a fund's price increased, and a negative number shows the price decreased. For instance, if a

Mutual fund tables are arranged alphabetically by the mutual fund company name, in bold. Following the company name are the vital statistics that explain the investment history of a fund.

mutual fund started at $19.75 and closed at $19.95, the net change was +0.20.

**YTD Chg** stands for year-to-date change, which displays how well a mutual fund has performed since the beginning of the year.

Like stocks, mutual funds are not guaranteed by the federal government. This is true even if someone buys them through a bank and the fund carries the bank's name. Mutual funds are popular investments for both beginning and experienced investors. Accounts are easy to set up, professional advice from experts is available, and the invested money is readily accessible, if needed.

# CHAPTER 6

# PUTTING IT TOGETHER

S ome professionals in the business world earn a living by telling people how to invest their money, when to invest it, and how much to invest. Many of these experts provide essential services and are valuable resources for their clients. However, no matter where any advice comes from, you are responsible for your own financial decisions.

## ABOUT BROKERS AND FINANCIAL ADVISERS

Everyone needs a broker to fill their orders to buy and sell bonds, stocks, and some mutual funds. Full-service, or traditional, brokerage firms work one on one with investors. In addition to making trades, they send regular account reports and often suggest other investments to their customers. People can reach their broker by telephone or e-mail. Some well-known, full-service brokerage companies include UBS, Wells Fargo Advisors, Merrill Lynch, and Morgan Stanley.

The interaction of a group discussion and decision usually creates a successful outcome. It is an excellent method for people to use when buying investments appropriate for their financial goals.

Individuals without much investing experience might want the advice of financial advisers, or planners, on the best way to save, invest, and grow their money. For example, advisers may recommend how to invest to reach a financial goal, such as paying for an education or buying a house. They can work with clients to develop a financial plan that fits their money goals, age, budget, and risk tolerance.

Older people may hire a certified financial planner (CFP) to create a long-term, comprehensive, personal finance plan

## FINDING A GOOD BROKER OR ADVISER

CHOOSING A TRUSTWORTHY BROKER OR FINANCIAL ADVISER IS ONE OF THE MOST IMPORTANT DECISIONS ANYONE CAN MAKE. AFTER ALL, THEY HELP PEOPLE TAKE CARE OF THEIR MONEY. BEGINNING INVESTORS CAN FIND LICENSED PROFESSIONALS BY CALLING A LOCAL BANK, A CREDIT UNION, OR AN INVESTMENT COMPANY. THEY SHOULD INTERVIEW SEVERAL BROKERS WITH THE SAME SET OF QUESTIONS AND THEN COMPARE THEIR ANSWERS. RELIABLE BROKERS AND ADVISERS WILL DISCUSS THEIR LICENSES, EDUCATION, AND EXPERIENCE. THEY SHOULD EXPLAIN THEIR SERVICES AND WHAT THEY COST, INCLUDING ALL FEES AND COMMISSIONS. COMPETENT FINANCIAL PROFESSIONALS ALSO PROVIDE REFERENCES. SAVVY INVESTORS CAN CHECK WITH THEIR STATE SECURITIES AGENCY TO MAKE SURE THAT A BROKER OR ADVISER IS LICENSED. THE NORTH AMERICAN SECURITIES ADMINISTRATORS ASSOCIATION WEBSITE (HTTP://WWW.NASAA .ORG) LISTS THE SECURITIES AGENCY FOR EVERY STATE.

for them. CFPs have specialized financial training. However, they are costly and probably not a good choice for young investors.

# ONLINE INVESTING

Online investing, or e-trading, is as easy as clicking a mouse or tapping on a mobile device. This method of investing is fast and convenient and works well for people who prefer doing their own research on which bonds, stocks, or mutual funds they want to buy or sell. When they are ready to place their order, they turn to discount brokers. These professionals do not provide the knowledge base or the advice that a full-service broker offers. However, their basic services cost less. They do this by eliminating the costs for branch offices and using computers to process trades.

When you pay lower commissions or fees on trades, more of your dollars are invested over time. Say someone only has $100 to buy stock, and a broker charges $1 for the purchase. That individual pays 1 percent of the $100 for the fee, leaving $99 for the original investment.

$$\$100 \times 1.00\% = \$1.00$$
$$\$100 - \$1 = \$99$$

If the person sells the stock, the broker may require another $1 for that transaction. Even using discount brokerage companies, these costs can quickly add up if an individual constantly buys and sells. Some reputable firms include Vanguard, Charles Schwab, TD Ameritrade, E*TRADE, Fidelity, Scottrade, Trade King, and Sharebuilder. Anyone can do online research and compare the services and fees of several different companies.

Electronic trading has drawbacks. Some electronic companies have limited products and services. Because investors do not have their own personal broker, reaching real staff to ask for help may be difficult. Online investing may encourage people to trade more than they should, which can result in

higher total costs and lower investment returns. In addition, they may be tempted to shift their money around and play all the angles. This can swamp smart investment planning. Wise investors take the time to research potential investments. They look for steady growth and long-term opportunities instead of daily wheeling and dealing. The attempt to buy and sell investments daily is called day trading.

# OPENING A BROKERAGE ACCOUNT

Creating and opening a brokerage account is a satisfying experience. Here are six basic steps to open a new account with a regular or discount broker:

1. Ask for a new brokerage account application from a bank, credit union, mutual fund company, investment company, or brokerage firm. Everyone needs to read this document carefully because it explains his or her legal rights on the account.
2. Answer all the questions on the form, including those about financial goals, income, investment experience, and risk tolerance. Brokers use this information to make future investment suggestions.
3. Make sure that you have complete control over all your investment decisions. A broker should not have the authority to buy or sell in your account without your permission.

---

Everyone needs a good grasp of online investing language to be successful. Investing books like this one and websites, such as Investopedia (www.investopedia.com) and InvestorWords (www.investorwords.com), are excellent resources.

4. Choose a cash account. Brokers use money deposited in this account to buy investments for their clients and pay their fees.

5. Sign the agreement and mail it or take it back to the broker. A parent or guardian must cosign for a minor.

6. After getting a copy of the agreement, deposit money into the new account. Many firms require $500, $1,000, or more to set up a new account.

For help with questions on the application, visit or call the bank, credit union, or brokerage firm, where experts are able to help you.

# THE NEXT BIG MOVE: PLACING A STOCK MARKET ORDER

It's a big step into the world of investing to buy your first stock. Many new investors feel excited and a bit nervous, even

Making your first stock purchase is significant. When you know what to expect, you will feel confident that your first investment experience will be positive.

if they are investing only a small amount. When people are ready to place an order, they see their broker in person, connect by telephone, or go online. Brokers are happy to help new investors through the process.

To actually buy stock, an order is placed with a broker or on an electronic account. A market order tells the broker or computer to buy shares of a stock at its current price. The transaction happens immediately.

# CHAPTER 7

# READY, SET, INVEST

All investors wish they could look into a crystal ball and see the future of bond, stock, or mutual fund markets. Although no one has that ability, everyone can do solid research to assess and buy investments that meet their budget and financial goals. Using sound strategies can

Even financial experts cannot offer crystal-ball gazing or other magic to foresee the markets. However, they can tell you that choosing sound investments takes time and effort.

help them grow their money faster than inflation and increase their purchasing power in the future.

# SENSIBLE STUDY: RESEARCH AND EVALUATION

Selecting good savings products and investments takes careful research and evaluation. Anyone can use the Internet to compare the current rates for savings accounts, money market accounts, and certificates of deposit at banks and credit unions. Bankrate is an excellent online source for this information.

Young people may turn to bond rating companies, such as Moody's Investors Service and Standard & Poor's, to study potential investments. These agencies score various bonds based on how well the government or corporation is doing financially. Bonds rated AAA or AA are the best because bondholders are highly likely to receive interest and have their loan repaid. Federal bonds are not graded because they are risk-free. The U.S. Treasury website posts the interest rates of federal bonds and how to purchase and redeem them.

When deciding which stocks to buy, potential investors might start by choosing a large restaurant or retail store that they like. Perhaps McDonald's, Wendy's, Apple, Microsoft, Nike, eBay, Wal-Mart, or Hershey come to mind. The stocks of these dependable companies usually increase in value and pay high dividends over time. Next, individuals can examine the Dow Jones Industrial Average, S&P 500, or other indices to see how well a corporation performed over the previous

year. They may dig for information by visiting the company's website and reading its quarterly reports and annual report. These documents describe the corporation's current finances and future goals.

Many people pick a mutual fund by first selecting a well-respected fund company, such as T. Rowe Price, Vanguard, Fidelity, or Charles Schwab. At the firm's website, they can read a fund's prospectus to learn more about it. An online research service, Morningstar Mutual Funds, provides valuable information on mutual funds.

More sources to research potential investments include business books and magazines at local libraries and bookstores, and websites. For example, Value Line is a respected online company that reviews the performance of many stocks and mutual funds. Other financial sites include Yahoo! Finance, MSN Money, and Standard & Poor's. Some business newspapers and magazines are in print and electronic formats, such as the *Wall Street Journal, Barron's, Forbes, Kiplinger's Personal Finance Magazine,* and *Smart Money.*

# FIGURING OUT AN INVESTMENT MIX

Most investors, including teens, usually want to know: What is the best mix of investments for me? The answer mostly depends on when they will need the money to meet their

For help determining which investments to buy and sell, keep track of local, national, and world news—especially news about business and the economy.

various financial objectives. People's tolerance to risk and age will also affect their decisions.

Suppose someone has a short-term goal of buying a new laptop for college in twelve months. The individual might buy short-term investments that act like cash but produce some interest. Good choices include money market accounts, short-term certificate of deposits (CDs), or Treasury bills.

With a longer period of time to invest, young people can take on a little more risk. For example, to purchase a new car in four years, they could consider four-year CDs, Treasury notes, or mutual funds that invest in blue-chip companies. These corporations pay high dividends and the value of their stock usually remains steady.

For even longer-term goals, such as buying a house in ten years, investors can think about long-term CDs, growth stocks, or growth stock mutual funds. Many financial counselors advise using index mutual funds, such as the S&P 500 index fund, as a method to invest in a wide variety of stock.

# PREPARING A PROFITABLE PORTFOLIO

Successful investors use an investment plan to generate wealth over time. They stick to a long-term, steady strategy. Everyone can use these five time-tested steps to make their dreams become reality:

1. Develop a financial plan, with saving and investing as top priorities. Savings build up money, and investing offers

the best way to achieve financial goals. The earlier young people commit to following these key concepts, the more money they can potentially generate over time.

2.  Invest a steady amount of money each month. Teens may want to add extra money into their long-term investments because, historically, the best way to increase wealth is by investing.

3.  Over time, build a diversified portfolio that includes different assets, such as bonds, stocks, and mutual funds. Wise investors know that the best investment strategy is to keep things simple. For example, they may own bond or stock mutual funds, instead of purchasing many individual bonds or stocks.

4.  Choose moderate-risk investments because they usually provide greater returns than conservative investments in the long run.

## JOIN THE (INVESTMENT) CLUB!

YOUNG PEOPLE MAY WANT TO JOIN AN INVESTMENT CLUB, WHICH IS OFTEN SPONSORED BY A LOCAL HIGH SCHOOL. EVERYONE WORKS TOGETHER TO MAKE MUTUAL DECISIONS ON INVESTING, ALTHOUGH SCHOOLS USUALLY PROHIBIT USING REAL MONEY. MEMBERS STUDY DIFFERENT BONDS, STOCKS, OR MUTUAL FUNDS AND MAKE REPORTS ON THEIR FINDINGS. EVERYONE IN THE GROUP JOINTLY VOTES TO BUY, SELL, OR KEEP VARIOUS PRODUCTS. PARTICIPATING IN AN INVESTMENT CLUB IS A GREAT WAY TO LEARN THE BASICS ABOUT WISE FINANCIAL PLANNING FOR THE FUTURE.

5.  Keep investing to meet new goals as your needs change over time. Investors should make continual, incremental purchases and not sell when the market value of their stocks or mutual funds temporarily declines.

Wealthy investors know that carefully selected bonds, stocks, and mutual funds have the potential to put money in their pocket. They can use those earned dollars to buy some of the same assets or buy more aggressive investment options.

# PRACTICE MAKES PERFECT

Some people may not be ready to invest real dollars, but they can still try stock trading with an imaginary account. To begin, they set up a logbook, starting with an initial investment of $1,000. Wise investors record all of their transactions because analyzing past decisions can help them understand their successes and mistakes. After researching several companies, they decide which stocks they would buy for their portfolio.

Next, they track the daily progress of their investments in a financial newspaper or online using a market index such as the Dow or S&P 500. They can sell a stock that is not performing well or might lose value soon, and buy a different one. In a month or two, they cash out and determine if they made a profit on their $1,000. This is a good way to practice for when they can invest with real money.

Successful trading is a learned behavior that demands knowledge and timely decisions. The best way to master trading is by purchasing imaginary stocks and tracking their value over time.

Another way to learn investing skills is on the Internet. Some websites offer free trading games that allow anyone to buy and sell stocks and follow what happens over time. Each investor starts with an imaginary amount of money, such as $25,000 or $100,000. Some sites to check out include Virtual Stock Exchange, Wall Street Survivor, UpDown, and optionsXpress.

# 10 GREAT QUESTIONS
## TO ASK A FINANCIAL ADVISER

1.  How much time will it take me to create my financial goals and plan?
2.  What are the best investments for me to meet my short-, medium-, and long-term goals?
3.  How do I determine my risk tolerance?
4.  What online services are available to help me learn how to manage my portfolio?
5.  How do I determine the amount of risk associated with an investment?
6.  What will cause the value of my stocks or mutual funds to rise or fall?
7.  I ordered my broker to make a trade but then changed my mind. What should I do?
8.  Should I ask a third party to review my portfolio once a year?
9.  My high school does not offer an investment club. How can I look into getting one started?
10. What financial records do I need to save from my investment accounts?

# CHAPTER 8

# STAYING ON TRACK

E veryone's future financial picture is determined by the actions they take today. Successful investing relies on solid money-management skills and learning how to avoid potential investment problems. Making investment decisions that are safe can mean a huge difference in achieving your goals.

## MANAGING FINANCIAL PLANS

A variety of tools are available for people to manage how they spend, save, and invest their money. Keeping track of their dollars can help people stick to their budget and investment plan and decide if they need to make changes to meet their goals. It does take time to set up and keep a system and then keep it up to date.

Everyone can determine what method works best for them. Paper and pencil work fine for some individuals. Other investors create a money-management system using word

Google Docs (docs.google.com) and Apache OpenOffice (www.openoffice.org) are examples of free software available on the Internet that offer basic worksheet programs for electronic money management.

processing or spreadsheet software. Smartphone apps are also available for this purpose. Others may prefer to use online services provided free by many banks, credit unions, investment companies, and mutual fund companies. This allows investors to track their money at any time by computer or smartphone.

Some websites provide free financial tools, such as Mint, Yodlee Money Center, and Personal Capital. These online programs help people plan and set up a budget and manage their finances. When investors log in to their accounts, all of their money activities are summarized in real time. They can view and evaluate their budgets, savings, and investment portfolios.

# PREVENTING INVESTMENT PROBLEMS

Everyone can take many steps to keep their money safe and reduce the chance of investment fraud. For instance, they can use a reputable company, such as Fidelity, Vanguard, Charles Schwab, T. Rowe Price, Dreyfus, or Wells Fargo, to handle their

## BEWARE! INVESTMENT FRAUDS AND SCAMS

YOU MIGHT SEE E-MAILS OR ONLINE ADS THAT PROMISE TO MAKE YOU A LOT OF CASH FAST. THESE FALSE PITCHES, OR "GET RICH SCHEMES," CAN INCLUDE BUYING RARE COINS, OIL WELLS, OR GOLD MINES. IF YOU FALL FOR THESE SCAMS, YOU PROBABLY WON'T GET ANY OF YOUR MONEY BACK. EVERYONE SHOULD FEEL WARY IF THEY ARE ENCOURAGED TO BORROW MONEY TO INVEST, FEEL PRESSURED TO ACT IMMEDIATELY, OR ARE PROMISED HIGH RETURNS WITHOUT ANY RISK. INVESTING ALWAYS ENTAILS TAKING RISKS. SPAM E-MAIL MIGHT CONTAIN PHONY OFFERS FOR INVESTMENTS THAT COULD END UP COSTING TIME AND MONEY. ALTHOUGH MOST E-MAIL PROGRAMS HAVE BUILT-IN SPAM FILTERS, SUSPICIOUS E-MAIL CAN BE MOVED, UNOPENED, TO A SPAM OR JUNK FOLDER.

When you write checks to a brokerage or financial services firm, a broker or an adviser can make purchasing decisions based on your instruction, but he or she can't disappear with your money.

financial accounts. People also need to write their checks or send any money to that business, not to an individual broker or financial adviser, and insist that they receive all investment confirmations and statements. Savvy investors review their statements regularly to verify the buying or selling prices, commissions, or fees on all transactions. This greatly reduces the opportunity for fraud.

If individuals see unauthorized trades on their account, they should call their broker or investment company immediately. Honest mistakes do occur. However, when complaints are not taken seriously, people may write a letter and send it to the company's manager or compliance officer. It's a good idea to file all of the correspondence on this matter in a safe place at home for future reference.

Another way to avoid scams is to check that investment professionals and their firms are registered with the U.S. Securities and Exchange Commission and licensed by the state to do business. The state regulatory agency posts this information and any disciplinary history of a broker or brokerage firm on its website. Unlicensed professionals are responsible for many investment frauds.

In spite of taking safety precautions, crooks might deceive people and steal their investment money. Although securities regulators and law enforcement officials can go after these thieves, they have limited resources to fight financial fraud. The best protection against being cheated is staying informed and making smart decisions about your money.

# PROTECTING ONLINE PRIVACY

Many people like the convenience of using the Internet to manage their budget and buy and sell investments. A disadvantage of these online services is that personal information may not be private or can be stolen. To help protect their privacy, everyone can look for and read the privacy statements on websites. They want to make sure companies do not sell details about customers to other companies. Policy statements are usually found on companies' websites in the "About" or "FAQ" section. These rules explain how a business protects any information that is collected.

71

Always use secure web pages when viewing financial accounts or making online transactions. Personal information on these sites is protected by password and kept safe by security technology, which makes it difficult to change or steal. An Internet address that begins with "https" or has an unbroken key or a closed lock to the left of the Internet address is a sign of a secure site.

When online, everyone needs to be careful about keeping and displaying their financial information. For example, they can limit the amount of personal information stored in their smartphone. Using the "key lock" function stops someone else from accessing their mobile devices. If a computer is not in use, it's a good idea to lock it. In addition, it's best to avoid making financial transactions on Wi-Fi offered in libraries, restaurants, retail stores, and other public places because personal information is not protected.

# BUILDING WEALTH

Investing might seem difficult at first, but it's not—especially if you make it a priority. Everyone can learn these skills from a treasure trove of resources, including print and digital information, investment clubs, economic teachers, personal bankers, and organizations such as the Boys and Girls Club of America, 4-H, and Junior Achievement. Some individuals may want to talk with a family member who is financially successful. Making good investment choices can help young people reach their long-term goals and lead to becoming wealthy. When teens follow their investment plan to reach financial milestones, they are taking control of their future.

**asset** Anything owned that can be converted into money, including bonds, stocks, and mutual funds.

**bond** A promise to pay a certain amount on a certain date, issued by a government or company, to borrow money.

**capital** The original amount of an investment.

**certificate of deposit (CD)** A savings account that pays interest based on a deposit for a specified length of time.

**commission** A fee charged by a broker for carrying out a transaction that is calculated as a percentage of the transaction value.

**compound interest** The amount earned on the original capital, plus the accumulated interest.

**diversify** To place money in several different types of investments.

**dividend** A portion of a company's profits paid to stockholders.

**fee** The price paid for services.

**inflation** The rising cost of goods and services.

**investing** The risking of money and time to get more money in return.

**issue** To create and sell bonds or stocks.

**market order** A trade made at the current market price. The stock is bought or sold as soon as the broker places the order.

**money market account** A type of savings account purchased through a bank or mutual fund company.

**mutual fund** An investment created and administered by financial professionals in which people pool their money to buy bonds, stocks, and other assets.

**portfolio** A group of investments owned by one person.

**profit** The money left over when something is sold for more than it was purchased.

**redeem** To cash in a bond.

**return** The earnings from a savings account or profit from an investment.

**risk** The possibility of loss.

**risk tolerance** The level of risk that a person is comfortable taking.

**securities** Any kind of financial investment that can be traded, such as stocks or bonds; a term for a variety of financial assets.

**share** A single piece of stock in a company or a unit of a mutual fund.

**stock** An investment in the ownership of a company.

**trade** The buying or selling of stocks.

**transaction** Any business, such as buying or selling investments.

Canadian Bankers Association (CBA)
Box 348
Commerce Court West
199 Bay Street, 30th Floor
Toronto, ON M5L 1G2
Canada
(800) 263-0231
Website: http://www.cba.ca
This association provides information for teens to learn about money, budgeting, investments, and banking in Canada.

Council for Economic Education
122 East 42nd Street, Suite 2600
New York, NY 10168
(800) 338-1192
Website: http://www.councilforeconed.org
The Council for Economic Education is an advocacy, research, and education organization that offers information on personal finances, including budgeting and investing.

Financial Planners Standards Council
902–375 University Avenue
Toronto, ON M5G 2J5
Canada
(800) 305-9886
Website: http://wwww.fpsccanada.org
The Financial Planners Standards Council provides information for teens on personal finance, budgeting, savings, investments, and more.

Jump$tart Coalition for Personal Financial Literacy
919 18th Street NW, Suite 300
Washington, DC 20006
(888) 45-EDUCATE (453-3822)
Website: http://www.jumpstart.org
Jump$tart supplies information on money management, budgeting, investing, and savings. Go to its clearinghouse to find a list of books and other print materials, CDs, DVDs, videos, and websites.

Securities and Exchange Commission
100 F Street NE
Washington, DC 20549
(800) 732-0330
Website: http://investor.gov
This federal agency provides help with investing and consumer protection questions.

# WEBSITES

Due to the changing nature of Internet links, Rosen Publishing has developed an online list of websites related to the subject of this book. This site is updated regularly. Please use this link to access the list:

http://www.rosenlinks.com/FSLS/Inves

Bamford, Jane. *Street Wise: A Guide for Teen Investors*. New York, NY: Bloomberg Press, 2010.

Butler, Tamsen. *The Complete Guide to Personal Finance: For Teenagers and College Students*. Ocala, FL: Atlantic Publishing Group, 2010.

Ferber, Kevin, and Mark Hansen. *Success 101 for Teens: Dollars and Sense for a Winning Financial Life*. St. Paul, MN: Paragon House, 2012.

Fryer, Julie. *The Teen's Ultimate Guide to Making Money When You Can't Get a Job: 199 Ideas for Earning Cash on Your Own*. Ocala, FL: Atlantic Publishing Group, 2012.

Gagne, Tammy. *Investment Options for Teens*. Hockessin, DE: Mitchell Lane Publishers, 2013.

Malkiel, Burton G., and Charles D. Ellis. *The Elements of Investing: Easy Lessons for Every Investor*. Hoboken, NJ: Wiley, 2013.

Merriman, Paul. *First-Time Investor: Grow and Protect Your Money*. Seattle, WA: CreateSpace, 2012.

Morrison, Jessica. *Investing*. New York, NY: Weigal Publishers, 2010.

O'Neal, Claire. *A Teen Guide to Buying Stocks*. Hockessin, DE: Mitchell Lane Publishers, 2013.

Stokes, Carol L. *Basic Beginnings: A Finance Management Handbook for Teens and Young Adults*. Seattle, WA: CreateSpace, 2010.

Stuver, Kent. *The Teen's Guide to Becoming a Millionaire*. Orem, UT: TG Empowerment Publications, 2012.

# BIBLIOGRAPHY

Center for Financial Literacy, Chaplin University. "2013 National Report Card." 2013. Retrieved August 14, 2013 (http://www.champlain.edu/Documents/Centers-of-Excellence/Center-for-Financial-Literacy/National-Report-Card-Champlain-College-CFL.pdf).

Heley, Logan. "Investment Tips for Teens." March 1, 2010. Retrieved August 1, 2013 (http://smeharbinger.net/features/investment-tips-for-teens).

Investment Company Institute. "Characteristics of Mutual Fund Owners." 2013. Retrieved August 14, 2013 (http://www.icifactbook.org/fb_ch6.html).

Krantz, Matt. *Investing Online for Dummies*. Hoboken, NJ: Wiley, 2012.

Kristof, Kathy. *Investing 101*. Hoboken, NJ: Bloomberg Press, 2010.

Quinn, Jane Bryant. *Making the Most of Your Money Now*. New York, NY: Simon & Schuster, 2009.

Teens Guide to Money. "Teens Guide to Investing." 2013. Retrieved August 4, 2013 (http://www.teensguideto money.com/investing).

U.S. Department of Labor. "Savings Fitness: A Guide to Your Money and Your Financial Fitness." 2008. Retrieved July 30, 2013 (http://www.dol.gov/ebsa/pdf/savingsfitness.pdf).

U.S. Securities and Exchange Commission. "Mutual Funds: A Guide for Investors." August 2007. Retrieved August 20, 2013 (http://investor.gov/sites/default/files/mutual-funds.pdf).

# INDEX

# ABOUT THE AUTHOR

Judy Monroe Peterson has earned two master's degrees and is the author of more than sixty educational books for young people. She is a former health care, technical, and academic librarian and college faculty member; a biologist and research scientist; and curriculum editor with more than thirty years of experience. She has taught courses at 3M, the University of Minnesota, and Lake Superior College. Currently, she is a writer and editor of K–12 and post–high school curriculum materials on a variety of subjects, including biology, life science, and the environment. She enjoys fishing for walleye with her family on the lakes of Minnesota.

# PHOTO CREDITS

Cover, p. 3 Gallo Images – LKIS/Getty Images; p. 6 JGI/Jamie Grill /Blend Images/Getty Images; p. 10 Tetra Images/Getty Images; p. 13 wrangler/Shutterstock.com; p. 16 pazzophoto/iStock/Thinkstock; p. 19 © David Young-Wolff/PhotoEdit; p. 22 Burke/Triolo Productions/Brand X Pictures/Thinkstock; p. 24 Jupiterimages/Photos.com/Thinkstock; p. 25 Dimitri Otis/Digital Vision/Getty Images; pp. 28, 37, 43 Bloomberg /Getty Images; p. 30 Stephen VanHorn/Shutterstock.com; p. 35 Hulton Archive/Archive Photos/Getty Images; p. 41 © AP Images; p. 47 Dragon Images/Shutterstock.com; p. 49 blackwaterimages/E+/Getty Images; p. 51 Steve Debenport/E+/Getty Images; p. 54 Kali Nine LLC/E+ /Getty Images; p. 56 Ridofranz/iStock/Thinkstock; p. 58 Peter vd Rol /Shutterstock.com; p. 60 © iStockphoto.com/Mixmike; p. 65 artpipi /E+/Getty Images; p. 68 Image Source/Getty Images; p. 70 Christopher Boswell/Shutterstock.com; interior page design elements © iStockphoto .com/ yystom (arrows), © iStockphoto.com/JLGutierrez (financial terms), © iStockphoto.com/ahlobystov (numbers).

Designer: Nelson Sá; Editor: Heather Moore Niver;
Photo Researcher: Cindy Reiman